Why

When Others' Approval Matters Too Much

Amy Baker

New
Growth
Press

newgrowthpress.com

New Growth Press, Greensboro, NC 27401
newgrowthpress.com

Cover Design: Tandem Creative, Tom Temple,
    tandemcreative.net
Typesetting: Lisa Parnell, lparnell.com

ISBN: 978-1-942572-41-1 (Print)
ISBN: 978-1-942572-42-8 (eBook)

Library of Congress Cataloging-in-Publication Data
    Names: Baker, Amy, 1959– author.
    Title: Why do I care? : when others' approval matters too
much / Amy Baker.
    Description: Greensboro, NC : New Growth Press, 2016.
    Identifiers: LCCN 2015040566 | ISBN 9781942572411
(pbk.) | ISBN 9781942572428 (ebook)
    Subjects: LCSH: Self-esteem—Religious aspects—
Christianity. | Self-acceptance—Religious aspects—
Christianity. | Social acceptance. | Integrity—Religious
aspects—Christianity.
    Classification: LCC BV4598.24 .B35 2016 | DDC 248.4—
dc23
    LC record available at http://lccn.loc.gov/2015040566

Printed in India

30 29 28 27 26 25 24 23   4 5 6 7 8

Daniel got wearily into his car for the twenty-minute drive home. Twenty minutes wasn't long enough to sort out his anxiety over his job being in jeopardy. Today his boss asked him to redesign his ad campaign to include more use of social media. Daniel was demoralized by his boss's remarks, interpreting his request as an indication that his boss was displeased with him and was looking for ways to get rid of him.

Daniel invests a lot of energy into trying to keep the approval of his bosses and colleagues. Sometimes this puts him in compromising positions. For example, his colleagues frequently repeat dirty or racist jokes. As a follower of Christ, Daniel doesn't enjoy hearing these off-color stories, but he listens and awkwardly laughs. He feels ashamed about laughing, but his fear of earning his coworkers' displeasure keeps him from speaking up or refusing to participate.

Later that evening when someone from his alma mater called and asked him to be part of a phone-a-thon for the university's capital campaign drive, Daniel agreed without even checking his schedule. When his wife Grace pointed out that they were supposed to be on vacation that week, Daniel brusquely responded that helping with the phone-a-thon was more important than vacation. He knew Grace was upset, but he needed to network in case he lost his job.

Daniel isn't usually aware of how driven he is to gain the approval of those around him. Nor does he realize that his fear causes him to misread others. In truth, his boss is not looking for ways to get rid of him; he simply wants a change in the advertising plan. Nevertheless, Daniel's fear of losing others' approval has caused him to perceive that his job is in danger. Living for the approval of others has become a way of life for him, and he invests time, energy, and emotion into making sure everyone in his world is pleased with him.

Even though she is upset about their vacation plans being ruined, Grace won't say anything to Daniel. Grace also lives for approval from others. She fears conflict will result in loss of Daniel's approval and possibly their marriage, so while she is internally angry that Daniel agreed to help with the phone-a-thon during their vacation, she keeps her anger to herself.

One small way Grace's desire for approval shows up is in her clothing choices. Grace puts a lot of time and energy into choosing what to wear, and it's not unusual for her to change her outfit multiple times before going somewhere. Grace equates others' approval of her wardrobe choices with their approval of her. She'll often try to collect data on her approval rating by asking innocuous questions like "Do you think these shoes go with this?" She is quietly testing the waters, hoping to hear an affirmation of her choice in order to lessen the tension she feels around others. Additionally, Grace often appears indecisive. If asked to state a preference, such as where she would like to go for lunch, Grace routinely tries to get someone else to make the choice so that she doesn't make a decision someone won't like.

Their daughter Amanda has learned her parents' ways, and she too tries to earn the approval of those around her. She is taking every advanced placement course she can in order to make it more likely that she will be accepted at the Ivy League school her parents and teachers want her to attend. She doesn't really care where she goes to school, but she knows her parents do. She doesn't want to disappoint them.

Although the studying required in AP classes leaves little time for social life, Amanda recently began dating a varsity basketball player. She enjoys the admiring glances of the other girls at school. However, her desire for popularity and approval are creating problems for her. Last weekend her boyfriend hinted that if she didn't have sex with him, he would break things off. Amanda doesn't want to have sex, but she fears that if she tells her new boyfriend no, he will break things off and she will lose her popularity among the other girls at school.

Daniel, Grace, and Amanda have all been fairly successful at cultivating the approval of those around them, but this hasn't brought them the peace and safety they hoped for. Instead, they still find themselves caught in the grip of anxiety, worried about the opinion of others, and fearful even when they get approval from others.

Perhaps you can relate to their struggles. The truth is that in our broken world we all are drawn toward hiding behind walls of success, accomplishment, and popularity to protect ourselves from rejection, displeasure, or humiliation. We crave the approval of others and can easily be overcome by what the Bible calls the fear of man. As a desire to please people becomes consuming, our lives become less and less authentic. That means that instead of loving people well and letting them know who we really are, we hide our real thoughts, feelings, and motives from others. Instead of getting to know them, we treat them as objects who should serve us by approving of everything we do. We don't get to know people and they don't get to know us. And fears that are not faced always grow. We start with wanting to please those closest to us, but we don't stop there. We long for everyone we encounter to approve of everything we do. This is a never-ending quest that is bound to end in disappointment. You have probably already experienced that disappointment and the fears that grow and consume your thought life.

This is a problem that affects everyone, but it's not unsolvable. There is a God who loves you and wants to help you. He has many things to say in his

Word about our fears and how to seek him for healing and peace.

Losing the Approval of Others Can Be Scary

It is difficult and sometimes frightening not to have the good opinion of others. At best, it's uncomfortable to have others think poorly of us. At worst, it's life-threatening. It is hard to face the possibility of rejection, humiliation, or opposition. We can tell people all day long that what others think of us doesn't matter. The problem is, *it does matter.* We want people to like us. We want others to be pleased with us. We want the approval of those around us.

Just like you, I struggle with people pleasing. If you simply told me to stop trying to please everyone, I would understand your point but not know how to apply it. It's so instinctive to me.

However, over the years the Spirit has taught me some things about getting beyond my desire to please others—and how to not let that desire control me. I have learned that although I want to be authentic, I often struggle and fail. I need help from outside myself. God is an ever-present help in trouble. He comes to my rescue and points me toward the help I need to get beyond my fear of people. Psalm 118 is one place in Scripture that has provided me help to love God and love people without fear.

Steps Toward Authenticity
from Psalm 118

Psalms 113–118 comprise a six-psalm praise to God sung at the Passover to celebrate the Jews' deliverance from Egypt. Traditionally, Psalm 113 and 114 were sung before the Passover meal and Psalm 115–118 afterward. Thus, Psalm 118 would most likely be what Christ and his disciples sang before they left the upper room the night Jesus was betrayed.[1] As Christ left the Last Supper to face the agonizing betrayal associated with his crucifixion, it is likely these words strengthened him for the rejection and suffering he was about to face. His sacrifice makes it possible for us to know love and acceptance that endures forever.

Meditate on God's love for you

One of the first steps we can take to be free of living for the approval of others is found in the beginning verses of Psalm 118.

> Give thanks to the LORD, for he is good;
>> his love endures forever.
> Let Israel say:
>> "His love endures forever."
> Let the house of Aaron say:
>> "His love endures forever."
> Let those who fear the LORD say:
>> "His love endures forever."
>
> (Psalm 118:1–4)

As people who love and long for approval, those who put their trust in God can rejoice in having received God's love and acceptance—a love and approval that will endure forever! This isn't what we deserve to get from the Lord. This psalm would make more sense from a human standpoint if we were to read, "Fear the Lord, for he is just and his wrath endures forever."

But Christ's willing sacrifice for our sins (he didn't die for any sins of his own) allowed God's wrath to be poured out on him instead of us. He was despised and rejected so we could be accepted by God. Now, those who belong to him receive God's full acceptance because Jesus died for us. When God looks at those who have trusted in Christ for salvation, he's able to look at us with eyes that see everything he loves about Jesus—the Son with whom he is well pleased. The rejection and wrath that should have been ours have been poured out on Jesus, and in its place we get God's love and acceptance.

Because "his love endures forever," we can take a step toward being less fearful of losing the approval of others. So, as verse 4 says, we need to be *saying* to ourselves, "his love endures forever."

Consider how rich and meaningful this is by repeating "his love endures forever" out loud four times, emphasizing a different word each time.

- *His* love endures forever. (Not the love of those whom we so desperately try to please in our jobs, our schools, our homes, and our social settings. *His* love is the love that endures.)
- His *love* endures forever. (His love, not his disapproval, his wrath, or his displeasure, endures forever.)
- His love *endures* forever. (His love isn't fickle. It isn't temporary. It won't wear out. It endures.)
- His love endures *forever*. (His love won't ever be lost. Unlike our peers, our children, or even our spouses, whose love it is possible to lose, his love endures *forever*.)

Cry out to God

> When hard pressed, I cried to the LORD;
>> he brought me into a spacious place.
>>> (Psalm 118:5)

Imagine what it would be like for Daniel to tell his coworkers he doesn't want to hear the jokes they tell. Think about how Grace would feel if others rejected her. Imagine how difficult it would be for Amanda to say no to sex with her boyfriend and be rejected by her boyfriend. Think about what it would be like in your life to lose approval from others.

It can be terribly hard to face losing the approval of others. Yet, organizing our lives around the approval of others confines us to a small world where life consists of trying to pleasing others so that we won't be rejected, humiliated, or exposed. We don't live freely in the big, wide world that God calls us to live in with love for him and love for others. Initially, we make choices we believe offer us protection, but in the end our fortress becomes our prison. The deception doesn't become apparent until the door has locked behind us and it no longer seems possible to choose anything but pleasing others. We end up living in a prison we've surrendered ourselves to in an attempt to find protection from the loss of approval.

So what can Daniel, Grace, and Amanda do? What can you or I do? We can do what the psalmist does in verse 5—we can cry out. We can tell the Lord about our anguish and fears. We can tell him how scared we are of being ridiculed, losing our job, being exposed, etc. We can cry out to the One whose love endures forever.

And when we cry out, what can we expect, according to verse 5? We can expect that God will answer and set us free! We can expect to be released from our prison cell of approval and brought to a spacious place.

Speak God's words to yourself

Psalm 118 continues by telling us what to do in our spacious place of freedom. Verses 6–7 explain that we need to redirect our attention from man to God.

> The Lord is with me; I will not be afraid.
> What can mere mortals do to me?
> The Lord is with me; he is my helper.
> I look in triumph on my enemies.
>   (Psalm 118:6–7)

We have to talk to ourselves, not just listen to our *fears*. It is easy for our thoughts to get caught up in the same old cycles that lead to the same choices and behaviors. So it is important to slow things down, recognize the thoughts that are running through our minds, and begin to interact with them.

Remind yourself that the Lord is with you. You are not alone. Even if the worst happens and others reject you, God hasn't. He is still with you. His love endures forever.

The psalmist asks, what can man, mere mortals, do? You might find you have a lot of intimidating answers to that question: people can reject me, hurt me, and even plot to take my life! And you're right. Any or all of those things could happen. But the psalmist couples this question with a declaration that the Lord is with him. He recognizes that while others can do extraordinarily hurtful things, he does not have to be ruled by fear. The Lord is with him, the Lord will help him, and his love endures forever.

As one who belongs to Christ, the same is true for you. He is calling you to a life of abundance where you are free to love others as Jesus did, regardless of how they respond. Instead of a fortress that keeps you trapped in a prison, your mighty Fortress goes with you out into the world. His love endures forever, and since you know from the Bible's great love chapter that love always protects (1 Corinthians 13:7), you can be confident that God will protect you from being crushed by the disapproval of others. And when Jesus returns, he will establish a kingdom where you will never again need to fear rejection, from God or others.

To overcome our fear of people, we will certainly have to talk with ourselves regularly, reminding ourselves that the Lord is with us and his love endures forever.

Trust the right people

Verses 8 and 9 give us details about how we talk with ourselves.

It is better to take refuge in the LORD
    than to trust in humans.
It is better to take refuge in the LORD
    than to trust in princes.
(Psalm 118:8–9)

It's better to trust in the Lord than to trust in people, even people who seem to be very powerful (like princes, or bosses, or varsity basketball players). Why? Partly because God can be trusted, but people are not always trustworthy. People who accept me today may reject me tomorrow. I can't trust that their love will endure forever. The girls at Amanda's school can't be trusted to admire her if she doesn't date her varsity basketball boyfriend. Daniel's boss can't be trusted to approve of him forever—that's why he is so worried. Grace doesn't trust that Daniel will love her if she disagrees with him. So it's best to take refuge in the Lord because his love endures forever.

But remember, part of trusting the Lord involves learning to develop relationships of trust with others. This is difficult to do if you're always trying to manage their responses because you're afraid of losing their approval. You must risk others' displeasure in order to build a deeper relationship with them. A good first step is to identify the people you're pretty sure will accept you no matter what. Then look for ways you are tempted to avoid, control, or escape situations that may lead to conflict with them. Ask God to help you step out in faith and love to be honest about your desires and feelings, and then do it! If they respond positively, take the time to appreciate that. Make it part of your mental landscape for when you are tempted to return to old patterns in the future.

If they respond negatively, don't assume that means you were wrong to try. You are learning to interact with others by faith, but that does not mean people will like it. They may have their own sinful patterns of relating that God is using *you* to address! Ultimately, another person's response is not the measure of whether you're on the right track. Trust in the Lord, follow the path he is setting for you, and he will be your refuge.

Recognize that victory is not dependent on my willpower

Suppose I have followed those steps and it just seems too hard. I don't think I can stand it anymore. Knowing that people are talking about me behind my back, ridiculing me, or eager to harm me seems overwhelmingly hard. The psalmist felt that way too. In verse 13 he tells us that he was pushed back and about to fall. It didn't feel like he was going to win. It felt like he was going to be defeated. But that's not what happened.

> I was pushed back and about to fall,
>> but the LORD helped me.
> The LORD is my strength and my defense;
>> he has become my salvation.
>>> (Psalm 118:13–14)

When I don't think I can take it anymore, I need to remind myself that victory is not dependent on my willpower. The Lord will help me. Therefore, I have hope!

Expect that if I follow these steps, joy will follow

> Shouts of joy and victory
>> resound in the tents of the righteous:
> "The LORD's right hand has done mighty
>> things!
>> The LORD's right hand is lifted high;
>> the LORD's right hand has done mighty
>> things!"
> I will not die but live,
>> and will proclaim what the LORD has done.
>> (Psalm 118:15–17)

It may be hard to keep going to God, to keep reminding myself of the truth of his love, but if you persevere, the Lord will do mighty things—in you and for you. Instead of being crushed by potential or actual loss of approval, you will be able to rejoice in what he does. You won't live in miserable silent despair, cut off from others; you will talk about what the Lord has done. You won't die, you will live.

What would it be like for Grace to experience victory over fear of what others think of her? Suppose she refrained from asking what her friends thought about her outfit even when she noticed her friend looking at her shoes. Suppose that she reminded herself that God's love endures forever and asked him to help her. When she was tempted to reply with her standard "I don't care. Where do you want to go?" when asked to select a place for lunch, suppose she told herself that God would help her and then decided where she would like to go.

Some of her friends may not like her choices and may choose not to associate with her much afterward. But not only will she feel more known and accepted by the friends who don't leave, but she will also be free of the burden of always trying to hit the moving target of what will be acceptable to the others.

Suppose Daniel reminded himself that God loves him and then told his coworkers he would prefer not to hear their off-color and racist stories. Suppose his coworkers reacted by asking if he thought he was better than them but Daniel quietly continued to work with his colleagues and put them in the best light possible to everyone around. He may be excluded from some groups at work, but his conscience will be clear before God and he may find that others respect him more.

Suppose Amanda told her varsity basketball boyfriend that she wouldn't have sex with him and she got dumped and ridiculed as a goody-two-shoes. Suppose she was shut out by girls that used to want her as a friend. She will have lost standing at her school, but she will no longer have to face pressure to go further physically than she wants and she will be able to find friends who respect her choices and accept her for who she is.

Taking bold steps like these would be incredibly hard, but the results can be surprising peace and joy.

What we thought would destroy us actually brings a victory. Of course, this will occur on the Lord's timetable, not ours—remember, the psalmist felt like he was about to fall. Following this pattern doesn't mean it will be easy, but it will equip us to endure and to see joy and victory.

Learn to look at the big picture

> The stone the builders rejected
>> has become the cornerstone;
> the LORD has done this,
>> and it is marvelous in our eyes.
> The LORD has done it this very day;
>> let us rejoice today and be glad.
>
> (Psalm 118:22–24)

When we fear or experience rejection from others, it's a big thing. Even if the rejection doesn't occur, our fear can produce as much anxiety (or more) as if the rejection actually occurred. But being rejected by others is not the whole story. When we live for approval, we focus only on what people can and may do to us. We don't see the big picture and our world becomes very small. We forget that God's love endures forever and we think we'll only be satisfied if we have the love or approval of those whose opinion we currently treasure. But verses 22–24 remind us of the bigger picture.

Christ was despised and rejected by men. He was a man of sorrows and familiar with suffering

(Isaiah 53:3). Yet, in God's world, things don't always turn out the way we think they will. At the cross, it seemed that Christ's rejection would result in eternal humiliation, but instead Christ has been exalted by God to the highest place and given the most respected name in the universe. God has determined that Christ is to have the highest approval rating of all time—every knee in heaven and on earth and under the earth will bow to him (Philippians 2:9–11).

As those who are united to Christ, we receive the benefits of his humiliation and exaltation. In him, we no longer have to fear ultimate humiliation and are able to move forward in faith, confident that we are accepted by God and will never be rejected. Things don't always turn out the way we fear they will. The Lord does marvelous things. Because of Christ we can rejoice today and be glad. Rejection, if it comes, will hurt but it won't last forever. God's love lasts forever.

We need to learn to look at the big picture. As we see God's big picture, it can be marvelous in our eyes. We can know that great things are on the horizon so we can rejoice and be glad *today*.

Repeat the process as necessary

> Lord, save us!
> Lord, grant us success!

Just because we work through these steps once doesn't mean we won't struggle with fear of people ever again. The psalmist may have repeated this process, as we perhaps see here in verse 25. We may find that the fear of others puts us in a stranglehold hours, minutes, or even seconds after we have followed the wisdom in Psalm 118. This is not our cue to give in and quit. This is our cue to remember that God's love endures forever and to persevere.

Remember to daily give more weight to God's love and approval than the approval and love of others

> You are my God, and I will praise you;
> > you are my God, and I will exalt you.
> > > (Psalm 118:28)

Of course, we all want the approval of both God and other people, and in God's kindness to us, it is often possible to have both. However, God also gives us opportunities to strengthen our faith by allowing occasions when we'll have to make choices regarding whose approval is more important to us. These will probably be hard situations. It won't be easy to show our loyalty to God, and we may find that we blow it, doing whatever it takes to have the approval of people.

But with God there is always forgiveness! At any moment that you notice you have lived for the approval of others instead of his love, you can turn to him and ask for forgiveness and help. Because of the cross and the resurrection, you can know that your forgiveness is guaranteed, along with a new start on your day.

As you learn to turn to God in repentance and faith, you will be training yourself to treasure God's love and approval more than the approval of others. At first, you will probably have to be mindful of this. When you begin to worry about what others think of you, you can consciously say to yourself, "It is better to have the Lord's approval than _____'s approval. Of course, I would like for everyone to like me, but if that's not possible, God's approval is worth much more to me than _____'s approval."

You will need to consciously say to God, "You are my God, and I will praise you; you are my God, and I will exalt you."

As you progress through this process, you'll begin to recognize after the fact times you blew it. You had an opportunity to show your loyalty to God and without even thinking about it, you chose to get the approval of others instead. However, God is faithful and he promises that if you repent and seek forgiveness, he will forgive.

Next, you may recognize that you have a chance to choose God's approval over the approval of others, but you'll choose to get the approval of others. This has been true in Daniel's life when he has wanted to quit listening to dirty jokes, but didn't use God's strength to speak up or walk away when they were told. Even so, Daniel can ask for God's forgiveness and be forgiven and given grace to change.

Finally, there may be awkward times in giving up the approval of others and taking steps to live for Jesus. For example, Daniel may blurt out "Stop!" when someone starts to tell him an off-color story. He may be so embarrassed that he doesn't know what else to say or do and his face may turn red. He may even wish he hadn't taken a stand. Nevertheless, he can rejoice because he has chosen to be loyal to Christ. He will learn that he can hold the pain of awkwardness or even rejection without being over-whelmed or destroyed by it because he places greater value on honoring Jesus than being approved by others.

As we falteringly practice these steps, over time we can expect to see God's harvest of peace bearing fruit in our lives. We should expect to see our anxiety decrease and our joy increase. Gradually it will become easier and easier to put verse 29 into practice.

Glorify God because his love and approval endure forever

Give thanks to the LORD, for he is good;
   his love endures forever.

(verse 29)

Psalm 118 ends in a crescendo of praise for the Lord. We are now prepared to give thanks to the Lord. We rejoice that he is good and trust in his forever-enduring love.

No Longer Dependent on Others' Approval

As we allow Psalm 118 to help us take steps toward authenticity, we can expect to see change take place. While we will still have a desire for approval, the desire is being restored to a proper place. Our primary desire is now a desire for the approval of God because we love him and want him to be glorified. Our joy is not dependent on others' approval, but finds a home in pleasing God because *his love endures forever.*

Living for the approval of others can become all-consuming and lead us to a place where we are captive to the opinions of others. Freedom begins as God rescues us through Christ and brings us into a spacious place—a place where his love endures forever. Because of this we can conclude that if God blesses us with the approval of men, we will thank God for it. On the other hand, if following God results in the displeasure of men, we will thank God that we have been worthy of suffering in his name (Acts 5:41). Our greatest treasure is our Lord, and we are confident in his love because his love endures forever.

Application Steps

1. Write out the Psalm 118 steps toward authenticity on several notecards and post them where you will see them frequently. Carry one of the notecards with you and put a small check beside any of the steps you take during the day. Each time you record a checkmark, give thanks to God for his grace and help.

2. While you are learning these new habits, consciously pause daily and thank God that his love endures forever. Set a goal to work toward doing this ten times a day. You might start by doing it before meals and at bedtime so it becomes more a part of your routine. This helps you to speak truth to yourself rather than merely listen to your fears.

3. Rather than focusing on how you can *get* love and approval from those around you, make a list of ways you can *give* love and godly approval to those folks. Then put one or two things from your list into practice each day.

4. For a more in-depth study, read Ed Welch's book, *When People Are Big and God Is Small*, or Lou Priolo's book, *Pleasing People*.

Endnotes

1. John MacArthur, *The MacArthur Bible Commentary* (Nashville, TN: Thomas Nelson, 2005), 675.